ICONS

TOKYO STYLE

TOKYO

Exteriors   Interiors

STYLE
Details

PHOTOS **Reto Guntli**
EDITOR **Angelika Taschen**

TASCHEN
HONGKONG KÖLN LONDON LOS ANGELES MADRID PARIS TOKYO

Front Cover: Plastic slats become "bamboo" screens in Kuma's design.
Couverture: Des lamelles en plastique se transforment en paravents de « bambou » sortis de l'imagination de Kengo Kuma.
Umschlagvorderseite: In Kumas Design werden Kunststofflatten zu »Bambus«-Wänden.

Back Cover: Neon overload: in the Shibuya district, Tokyo.
Dos de Couverture: Surabondance de néons : le quartier de Shibuya, à Tokyo.
Umschlagrückseite: Neon über Neon im Shibuya-Bezirk von Tokio.

Also available from TASCHEN:

Inside Asia
2 volumes, 880 pages
ISBN-10: 3-8228-1441-5
ISBN-13: 978-3-8228-1441-3

To stay informed about upcoming TASCHEN titles, please request our magazine
at www.taschen.com/magazine or write to TASCHEN, Hohenzollernring 53, D-50672 Cologne,
Germany, contact@taschen.com, Fax: +49-221-254919. We will be happy to send you a free copy
of our magazine which is filled with information about all of our books.

© 2006 TASCHEN GmbH
Hohenzollernring 53, D-50672 Köln
www.taschen.com

Concept, layout and editing by Angelika Taschen, Berlin
Project management by Stephanie Bischoff, Cologne
Texts by Daisann McLane, Hong Kong
Lithography by Thomas Grell, Cologne
German translation by Anne Brauner, Cologne
French translation by Carine Mathey for mot.tiff, Paris

Printed in Italy
ISBN-10: 3-8228-1006-1
ISBN-13: 978-3-8228-1006-4

CONTENTS SOMMAIRE INHALT

Tokyo, alone among the world's great metropolises, is a city without an icon. New York and Hong Kong have their famous skylines, Paris its Eiffel Tower, London its bridges across the Thames. Tokyo has no signature buildings, no skyline, no stunning harbours or rivers. In the popular imagination, Tokyo exists as a sprawl, amorphous and constantly changing. Its most famous representation is not real, but cinematic: Tokyo is the movie set through which Godzilla stomps and rampages. The cycle of destruction, rebuilding and transformation defines a city that reveals itself not in its permanent structures, but in its plasticity, in the creativity of its constant changes. There are important historical and geographical reasons why Tokyo is the world's Plastic City. Located atop the volatile Pacific Rim, Tokyo has been destroyed several times by earthquake and fire. The bombings of World War II flattened whole swaths of the city, and nowadays, global warming seems to

PLASTIC CITY

Parmi les plus grandes métropoles du monde, Tokyo est la seule à ne pas avoir d'icône symbolique. New York et Hong-Kong sont réputées pour leurs gratte-ciel, Paris pour sa tour Eiffel et Londres pour ses ponts au-dessus de la Tamise. Tokyo ne possède ni bâtiment caractéristique ni horizon célèbre, ni port ni rivière remarquable. Dans l'imaginaire populaire, Tokyo apparaît comme une vaste étendue amorphe, en perpétuelle évolution. Sa représentation la plus célèbre n'est pas réelle, mais cinématographique : Tokyo est le décor que Godzilla piétine en laissant éclater sa fureur. Cette ville, révélée non pas à travers ses structures permanentes, mais dans sa plasticité et dans la créativité de ses éternelles métamorphoses, se définit par un cycle de destruction, de reconstruction et de transformation. D'importants facteurs historiques et géographiques expliquent le fait que Tokyo ait reçu le surnom de « ville plastique ». En raison de sa situation critique en bordure du Pacifique, Tokyo a été détruite plusieurs fois par des tremblements de terre et des incendies. Les bombardements de la Seconde Guerre mondiale ont rasé des quartiers entiers de la ville, et

Unter den großen Metropolen der Welt ist Tokio die einzige ohne eigenes Wahrzeichen. New York und Hongkong präsentieren ihre berühmten Skylines, Paris den Eiffelturm und London die Brücken über die Themse. Tokio verfügt weder über Gebäude, eine Skyline noch über Häfen, an denen man die Stadt erkennen könnte. In der allgemeinen Vorstellung existiert Tokio als ausuferndes, formloses Gebiet, das in stetigem Wandel begriffen ist. Die berühmteste Darstellung entspringt nicht der Wirklichkeit, sondern einem Film: Godzilla wütet und rast vor der Kulisse Tokios. Der Zyklus aus Zerstörung, Wiederaufbau und Wandel beschreibt eine Stadt, die sich nicht in bleibenden Strukturen enthüllt, sondern in ihrer Formbarkeit und der schöpferischen Kraft permanenter Veränderung. Bedeutende historische und geografische Entwicklungen begründen Tokios Ruf als die Plastic City unserer Welt. Aufgrund seiner Lage im volatilen pazifischen Randgebiet wurde Tokio mehrmals durch Feuer und Erdbeben zerstört. Im Zweiten Weltkrieg legten die Bomben ganze Stadtviertel in Schutt und Asche, während heutzutage die globale Erwärmung zu einer Zunahme der Taifune führt, die über das

be sending even more typhoons up the Sea of Japan in Tokyo's direction. Is it possible to make a home, find a personal style, in the midst of such impermanence and volatility? The answer to that question can be found in the pictures in the following pages. From the houses that take advantage of every square centimeter of precious Tokyo living space, to the concrete hotels shaped like overgrown toy robots, Tokyo architects and designers are masters at putting a human face and scale on their creations. They embrace the new, the experimental, the avant-garde in everything from their choice of materials to the way they re-organize and re-conceptualize living space. But in the bathroom there is always a nice deep traditional Japanese tub to soak away the aches and pains of post-modernity. In a Tokyo house made entirely of plastic, soft diffused sunlight creates a play of shadows on the polyethylene wall, as elegant as a Geisha's silhouette on a rice paper Shoji screen.

aujourd'hui, le réchauffement de la planète semble être à l'origine du nombre croissant des typhons qui se forment dans la mer du Japon en direction de Tokyo. Est-il possible de bâtir et de trouver un style personnel au milieu de tant de fugacité et d'instabilité ? La réponse à cette question se trouve dans les illustrations du présent ouvrage. Des maisons exploitant chaque centimètre carré de la précieuse surface habitable de la métropole aux hôtels en béton dont les formes rappellent celles de gigantesques robots, les architectes et designers de Tokyo sont passés maîtres dans l'art d'humaniser leurs créations. Ils sont adeptes de la nouveauté, de l'expérimental et de l'avant-garde, depuis le choix du matériau jusqu'à la manière dont ils conceptualisent et réorganisent l'espace de vie. Ce qui n'empêche pas de retrouver dans la salle de bain la traditionnelle baignoire japonaise dont la profondeur nous fait oublier les maux de la post-modernité… Dans une maison de Tokyo entièrement réalisée en plastique, la lumière du soleil tamisée crée un délicat jeu d'ombres sur le mur en polyéthylène, aussi élégant que la silhouette d'une geisha sur un paravent Shoji en papier de riz.

Japanische Meer in Richtung Tokio ziehen. Kann man inmitten solcher Unbeständigkeit und Volatilität ein Heim schaffen und zu einem eigenen Stil finden? Die Antwort auf diese Frage geben die Bilder auf den folgenden Seiten. Von Häusern, die jeden Quadratzentimeter des kostbaren Tokioter Lebensraums ausnutzen, bis zu den Hotels aus Beton, die wie zu groß geratene Roboter wirken, zeigt sich die Meisterschaft der Architekten und Designer aus Tokio darin, dass sie ihren Werken menschliche Züge und Maße verleihen. Sie machen sich das Neue, das Experimentelle und die Avantgarde zu eigen, sei es bei der Wahl des Baumaterials oder der Art, wie sie den Lebensraum neu organisieren und entwerfen. Doch in jedem Badezimmer findet sich noch immer ein tiefes traditionelles Badebecken, in dem sich die Schmerzen und Mühen der Postmoderne lösen. In einem Haus in Tokio, das vollständig aus Kunststoff errichtet wurde, wirft diffuser Sonnenschein Schattenspiele an die Wand aus Polykarbonat – elegant wie die Silhouette einer Geisha auf einer Shoji-Schiebetür aus Reispapier.

"...We live in a world where great incompatibles co-exist: the human scale and the superhuman scale, stability and mobility, permanence and change, identity and anonymity, comprehensibility and universality..."

Kenzo Tange, *Architect, Japan*

«...Nous vivons dans un monde où coexistent des éléments hautement incompatibles : échelle humaine et surhumaine, stabilité et mobilité, permanence et changement, identité et anonymat, intelligibilité et universalité...»

Kenzo Tange, *Architecte, Japon*

»...Wir leben in einer Welt, in der viele Gegensätze nebeneinander existieren: Die menschliche und die übermenschliche Ebene, Stabilität und Mobilität, Beständigkeit und Wandel, Identität und Anonymität, Verständlichkeit und Universalität...«

Kenzo Tange, *Architekt, Japan*

EXTERIORS

Extérieurs   Aussichten

10/11 Urban dynamo: bird's-eye view of Tokyo's Shinjuku district. *Centre urbain : vue panoramique du quartier de Shinjuku, à Tokyo.* Dynamik in der Stadt: Der Shinjuku-Bezirk in Tokio aus der Vogelperspektive.

12/13 Another perspective on Tokyo, from the Park Hyatt Hotel. *Tokyo, vue d'une autre perpective, depuis l'hôtel Park Hyatt.* Eine weitere Aussicht auf Tokio, vom Park Hyatt Hotel.

14/15 Dawn breaks over Shinjuku, at the Park Hyatt. *Lever du soleil au-dessus du quartier de Shinjuku, depuis l'hôtel Park Hyatt.* Sonnenaufgang über Shinjuku am Park Hyatt.

16/17 Neon overload: in the Shibuya district, Tokyo. *Surabondance de néons : le quartier de Shibuya, à Tokyo.* Neon über Neon im Shibuya-Bezirk von Tokio.

18/19 Building or robot? Night view of Tokyo's Sofitel Hotel. *Architecture ou technologie ? Vue nocturne de l'hôtel Sofitel, à Tokyo.* Gebäude oder Roboter? Nachtansicht des Sofitel Hotels in Tokio.

20/21 Tokyo's Ueno Park, from the roof of the Sofitel. *Le parc d'Ueno, vu du toit de l'hôtel Sofitel.* Der Ueno-Park in Tokio, Aussicht vom Dach des Sofitel Hotels.

22/23 A balcony at the Sofitel Hotel, Tokyo. *Un balcon de l'hôtel Sofitel, à Tokyo.* Ein Balkon des Sofitel Hotels in Tokio.

24/25 Study in contrast: the Sofitel and a garden pagoda, Ueno Park. *Jeu de contrastes : l'hôtel Sofitel derrière une pagode du parc d'Ueno.* Kontrastprogramm: Das Sofitel und eine Gartenpagode im Ueno-Park.

26/27 Sparkle and glitz: rooftop at Claska Hotel, Tokyo. *Faste et éclat : toit de l'hôtel Claska, à Tokyo.* Glanz und Glitter auf dem Dach des Claska Hotels in Tokio.

28/29 Modernist facade of Tokyo's Claska, a boutique hotel. *Modernisme de la façade de l'hôtel-boutique Claska, à Tokyo.* Modernistische Fassade des Boutiquehotels Claska.

30/31 Urban oasis: roof terrace at the Claska Hotel. *Oasis urbaine : terrasse sur le toit de l'hôtel Claska.* Oase in der Stadt: Die Dachterrasse des Claska Hotels.

32/33 Rooftop chill-out space, Claska Hotel, Tokyo. *Espace détente sur le toit de l'hôtel Claska, à Tokyo.* Chillout auf dem Dach des Claska Hotels in Tokio.

34/35 Exterior platform of Kenzo Kuma's Plastic House, Tokyo. *Terrasse extérieure de la Maison de Plastique de Kengo Kuma, à Tokyo.* Außenplattform am Plastic House von Kenzo Kuma in Tokio.

36/37 Kuma's Plastic House is made from fiberglass reinforced polymer. *La Maison de Plastique de Kuma, réalisée en polymère renforcé de fibres de verre.* Kumas Plastic House wurde aus fiberglasverstärktem Kunststoff erbaut.

38/39 Balcony at Eizo Shiina's suburban Tokyo house. *Balcon de la résidence d'Eizo Shiina, dans la banlieue de Tokyo.* Balkon an Eizo Shiinas Haus in einem Außenbezirk Tokios.

40/41 Triangular window, in architect Eizo Shiina's house. *Fenêtre triangulaire, dans la maison de l'architecte Eizo Shiina.* Dreieckiges Fenster im Haus von Eizo Shiina.

42/43 Sweeping urban view from designer Junko Koshino's apartment. *Vue panoramique de la ville, depuis l'appartement du designer Junko Koshino.* Junko Koshinos Wohnung bietet einen weiten Ausblick auf die Stadt.

44/45 Stunning Tokyo views dominate Koshino's open-plan living space. *L'espace de vie ouvert de Junko Koshino, dominé par des vues imprenables sur Tokyo.* Die wunderbare Aussicht auf Tokio beherrscht Koshinos offenen Wohnbereich.

"…The lifespan of a building has nothing to do with the materials. It depends on what people do with it. If a building is loved, then it becomes permanent. When it is not loved, even a concrete building can be temporary…"

Shigeru Ban, *Architect, Japan*

«…La durée de vie d'un bâtiment n'a rien à voir avec les matériaux utilisés. Elle dépend de l'usage qu'en font les gens. Un bâtiment aimé devient éternel. Si on ne l'aime pas, même un bâtiment en béton peut être éphémère…»

Shigeru Ban, *Architecte, Japon*

»…Die Lebensdauer eines Gebäudes hängt nicht vom Baumaterial ab, sondern davon, wie die Menschen damit umgehen. Wird ein Gebäude geliebt, bleibt es bestehen. Wird es nicht geliebt, kann auch ein Betonbau vergehen…«

Shigeru Ban, *Architekt, Japan*

INTERIORS

Intérieurs   Einsichten

50/51 Stylish retreat: sitting area, Yoshifumi Nakamura's house, Tokyo. *Refuge élégant : salon de la demeure de Yoshifumi Nakamura, à Tokyo.* Stilvolle Rückzugsmöglichkeit: Lese-ecke in Yoshifumi Nakamuras Haus in Tokio.

52/53 Natural wood and light add warmth to the Nakamura house, Tokyo. *Le bois naturel et la lumière donnent une atmosphère chaleureuse à la maison de Yoshifumi Nakamura, à Tokyo.* Naturhölzer und Licht verleihen Nakamuras Haus in Tokio eine warme Ausstrahlung.

54/55 Cozy nook: a built-in sofa at Nakamura's house, Tokyo. *Coin confortable : canapé encastré dans la maison de Yoshifumi Nakamura, à Tokyo.* Auf dem eingebauten Ruhebett in Nakamuras Haus in Tokio kann man es sich gemütlich machen.

56/57 Space matters: another quiet corner in the Nakamura house, Tokyo. *Importance de l'espace : un autre coin tranquille de la maison de Yoshifumi Nakamura, à Tokyo.* Der Raum spielt eine große Rolle: Eine weitere Oase der Ruhe in Nakamuras Haus in Tokio.

58/59 Natural teak counters and cabinets in the Nakamura's kitchen. *Teck naturel pour le comptoir et les meubles de la cuisine de Yoshifumi Nakamura.* Theken und Schränke aus naturbelassenem Teakholz in der Küche des Nakamura-Hauses in Tokio.

60/61 A traditional Japanese cedar soaking tub in the Nakamura bathroom. *Baignoire japonaise traditionnelle en cèdre, dans la salle de bain de Yoshifumi Nakamura.* Das traditionelle Bade-becken im Badezimmer des Nakamura-Hauses wurde aus Zedernholz gefertigt.

62/63 Lost in Translation: the library at Kenzo Tange's Park Hyatt Hotel. *Lost in Translation : la bibliothèque de l'hôtel Park Hyatt conçu par Kenzo Tange.* Lost in Translation: die Biblio-thek in Kenzo Tanges Park Hyatt Hotel.

64/65 Bamboo breakfasts: dining space at Park Hyatt Hotel. *Ambiance bambou : salle de restaurant de l'hôtel Park Hyatt.* Frühstück unter Bambus: Der Speisesaal des Park Hyatt Hotels.

66/67 Dramatic vistas of Tokyo in the mod-ernist lounge, Park Hyatt Hotel. *Vues spec-taculaires de Tokyo depuis le salon moderniste de l'hôtel Park Hyatt.* Atemberaubende Ausblicke auf Tokio von der modernistischen Lounge des Park Hyatt Hotels.

68/69 Smooth as glass: reflections of Tokyo in the Park Hyatt swimming pool. *Aussi lisse que le verre : reflets de Tokyo dans la piscine de l'hôtel Park Hyatt.* Glatt wie Glas: Tokio spiegelt sich im Swimmingpool des Park Hyatt.

70/71 Drinks on the rooftop at Tokyo's boutique Claska Hotel. *Espace détente sur le toit de l'hôtel-boutique Claska, à Tokyo.* Drinks auf dem Dach des Tokioter Boutiquehotels Claska.

72/73 Lounge at the Claska Hotel, which opened in 2003. *Salon de l'hôtel Claska inauguré en 2003.* Die Lounge des Claska Hotels, das 2003 eröffnet wurde.

74/75 The Claska Hotel bar has a retro feel and a dj beat. *Ambiance rétro et rythmée par un D.J. pour le bar de l'hôtel Claska.* In der Bar des Claska Hotels genießt man Retrodesign zu DJ-Klängen.

76/77 Another perspective on the modern bar-lounge at the Claska Hotel. *Autre vue du bar-salon moderne de l'hôtel Claska.* Eine weitere Aufnahme der modernen Lounge-Bar des Claska Hotels.

78/79 At "essence": the Claska Hotel's reading room and bookstore. *Librairie et salle de lecture de l'hôtel Claska.* Auf das Wesentliche reduziert: Der Lesesaal und die Buchhandlung des Claska Hotels.

80/81 Simple and elegant: one of the Claska Hotel's nine guestrooms. *Simplicité et élégance : l'une des neuf chambres de l'hôtel Claska.* Schlichte Eleganz: Eines der neun Zimmer des Claska Hotels.

82/83 Cool comfort: another guestroom at Tokyo's Claska Hotel. *Confort et détente : autre chambre de l'hôtel Claska, à Tokyo.* Bequem und cool: Ein weiteres Zimmer des Claska Hotels in Tokio.

84/85 Recessed shelves hold ceramic treasures: Junko Koshino's kitchen. *Trésors en céramiques sur des étagères encastrées, dans la cuisine de Junko Koshino.* Die Einbauschränke beherbergen kostbare Keramik: Junko Koshinos Küche.

86/87 Modern serenity: tea ceremony room in Koshino's flat, Tokyo. *Sérénité moderne : salle consacrée à la cérémonie du thé dans l'appartement de Junko Koshino, à Tokyo.* Moderne Gelassenheit: Der Raum für die Teezeremonie in Koshinos Wohnung in Tokio.

88/89 Tokyo sunset from the open-plan living area, Koshino's flat. *Coucher de soleil sur Tokyo depuis l'espace de vie ouvert de l'appartement de Junko Koshino.* Sonnenuntergang in Tokio: Aussicht aus dem offenen Wohnbereich in Koshinos Wohnung.

90/91 A floating world: Koshino's apartment, high above Tokyo. *Un monde flottant : l'appartement de Junko Koshino surplombe Tokyo.* Schwebende Welten: Koshinos Wohnung hoch oben über Tokio.

92/93 Serenity: a glass-enclosed atrium in Koshino's apartment, Tokyo. *Sérénité : cour intérieure aux murs de verre dans l'appartement de Junko Koshino, à Tokyo.* Gelassenheit: Tafelglas umrahmt das Atrium in Koshinos Wohnung in Tokio.

94/95 Urban tension and dramatic beauty: Koshino's open living space. *Tension urbaine et beauté dramatique : l'espace de vie ouvert de Junko Koshino.* Die Anspannung der Stadt kombiniert mit dramatischer Schönheit: Koshinos offener Wohnraum.

96/97 Living room and garden-like bathroom, Eizo Shiina's house. *Salon et salle de bain aux allures de jardin, dans la maison d'Eizo Shiina.* Wohnzimmer und gartenartiges Bad in Eizo Shiinas Haus.

98/99 Concrete walls hide a traditional soaking tub at Shiina's house. *Des murs de béton dissimulent une baignoire traditionnelle dans la maison d'Eizo Shiina.* In Shiinas Haus verbirgt sich ein traditionelles Badebecken hinter Betonwänden.

100/101 Guardian diety: the central fireplace at Eizo Shiina's. *Figure protectrice : cheminée centrale, chez Eizo Shiina.* Die zentrale Feuerstelle wirkt in Eizo Shiinas Haus wie eine »Schutzgöttin«.

102/103 Concrete meets steel: in Eizo Shiina's kitchen. *Rencontre du béton et de l'acier : la cuisine d'Eizo Shiina.* Beton kombiniert mit Edelstahl: Eizo Shiinas Küche.

104/105 Outside, looking in: at Kengo Kuma's Plastic House. *Depuis l'extérieur, aperçu de l'intérieur de la Maison de Plastique de Kengo Kuma.* Einblick von draußen in Kengo Kumas Plastic House.

106/107 Plastic filters and diffuses the light inside Kuma's Plastic House. *La lumière est tamisée et diffusée par le plastique à l'intérieur de la Maison de Plastique de Kuma.* Der Kunststoff filtert und verteilt das Licht in Kumas Plastic House.

108/109 Monochromatic, modern: living room in Kuma's Plastic House. *Monochromatisme et modernité : salon de la Maison de Plastique de Kuma.* Einfarbig modern: Der Wohnbereich in Kumas Plastic House.

110/111 Plastic slats become "bamboo" screens in Kuma's design. *Des lamelles en plastique se transforment en paravents de « bambou » sortis de l'imagination de Kengo Kuma.* In Kumas Design werden Kunststofflatten zu »Bambus«-Wänden.

112/113 Celadon glow: morning in the kitchen of the Plastic House. *Lueur vert céladon : le matin dans la cuisine de la Maison de Plastique.* Seladongrünes Leuchten: Morgens in der Küche des Plastic House.

114/115 See through: a clear plastic chair accents Plastic House's bath. *Transparence : une chaise en plastique translucide met en valeur la salle de bain de la Maison de Plastique.* Durchsichtig: Ein transparenter Kunststoffstuhl setzt Akzente im Badezimmer des Plastic House.

116/117 The plastic panels resemble traditional screens, Plastic House. *Panneaux de plastique ressemblant à des paravents traditionnels, dans la Maison de Plastique.* Die Kunststoffwände im Plastic House ähneln den traditionellen Trennwänden.

118/119 Architect Masaki Endo's Natural Strips II house, only 85 meters square. *La maison Natural Strips II de l'architecte Masaki Endo, d'une superficie de 85 m² seulement.* Das Natural-Strips-II-Haus des Architekten Masaki Endo nimmt nur 85 Quadratmeter ein.

120/121 Clean and compact: the kitchen at Endo's Natural Strips II house. *Nette et compacte : la cuisine de la maison de Masaki Endo.* Sauber und kompakt: Die Küche in Endos Natural-Strips-II-Haus.

122/123 Monochrome colors, simple living: at Natural Strips II house. *Couleurs monochromes et simplicité pour la maison de Masaki Endo.* Die Einfarbigkeit betont die schlichte Lebensart im Natural-Strips-II-Haus.

124/125 Tiny outdoor patio: Natural Strips II house, Tokyo. *Minuscule cour extérieure de la maison de Masaki Endo, à Tokyo.* Das Natural-Strips-II-Haus in Tokio verfügt über einen winzigen Patio im Freien.

"...The role of tradition is that of a catalyst which furthers a chemical reaction, but is no longer detectable in the end result..."

Kenzo Tange, *Architect, Japan*

«...La tradition a un rôle de catalyseur destiné à favoriser une réaction chimique, indétectable dans le résultat final...»

Kenzo Tange, *Architecte, Japon*

»...Tradition wirkt wie ein Kataklysmus, der eine chemische Reaktion auslöst, die jedoch im Endergebnis nicht mehr nachzuweisen ist...«

Kenzo Tange, *Architekt, Japan*

DETAILS

Détails   Details

手造り黒麹かめ仕込み
沈村麦香

本格焼酎
蜜酒の杯
秘蔵の酒

㊙
かめ仕込本格焼酎
杜の妖精
もりのようせい

本格焼酎
酉美々香
すいびくか

132 Bottles of premium sake, bar at Claska Hotel, Tokyo. *Bouteilles de saké de premier choix, dans le bar de l'hôtel Claska, à Tokyo.* Flaschen erstklassigen Sakes in der Bar des Claska Hotels in Tokio.

134 Detail, the lounge-bar of the Claska Hotel. *Détail du bar-salon de l'hôtel Claska.* Detail, die Lounge-Bar des Claska Hotels.

135 Cool tubes: Modern light fixtures at the Claska Hotel bar. *Tubes originaux : luminaires modernes dans le bar de l'hôtel Claska.* Kühle Röhren: Moderne Lichtgestaltung in der Bar des Claska Hotels.

137 Reading nook at Yoshifuma Nakamura's house, Tokyo. *Coin lecture dans la maison de Yoshifumi Nakamura, à Tokyo.* Eine Leseecke in Yoshifuma Nakamura's Haus in Tokio.

138 Another view of the reading nook, Nakamura's house, Tokyo. *Autre vue du coin lecture de la maison de Yoshifumi Nakamura, à Tokyo.* Die Leseecke des Nakamura-Hauses in Tokio aus einer anderen Perspektive.

139 Restful repose: a corner for naps at Nakamura's house. *Repos et délassement : coin sieste dans la maison de Yoshifumi Nakamura.* Ein Ort der Ruhe in Nakamuras Haus: Ideal für ein kleines Nickerchen.

141 Detail, guest room at Kenzo Tange's Park Hyatt Hotel. *Détail d'une chambre de l'hôtel Park Hyatt de Kenzo Tange.* Detail, Hotelzimmer in Kenzo Tanges Park Hyatt Hotel.

142 The study at Yoshifuma Nakamura's house, Tokyo. *Le bureau de la demeure de Yoshifumi Nakamura, à Tokyo.* Das Arbeitszimmer in Yoshifuma Nakamuras Haus in Tokio.

143 Retro-look bike outside the Claska Hotel, Meguru-dori, Tokyo. *Un vélo au design rétro devant l'hôtel Claska, dans la Meguro-dori, à Tokyo.* Ein Fahrrad im Retro-look vor dem Claska Hotel, Meguru-dori, Tokio.

144 Interior detail of the 9-room Claska Hotel, Tokyo. *Détail intérieur de l'hôtel Claska aux neuf chambres, à Tokyo.* Innenarchitektonisches Detail im Claska Hotel, Tokio, das über neun Hotelzimmer verfügt.

146 Red antique boxes in the Nakamura house, Tokyo. *Boîtes rouges anciennes dans la maison de Yoshifumi Nakamura, à Tokyo.* Antike rote Kästen in Nakamura-Haus in Tokio.

147 Tempting desserts at the buffet, Park Hyatt Hotel, Tokyo. *Tentation des desserts du buffet de l'hôtel Park Hyatt, à Tokyo.* Verführerische Desserts am Büffet des Park Hyatt Hotels in Tokio.

148 Drinks on the rooftop, Claska Hotel, Tokyo. *Espace détente sur le toit de l'hôtel Claska, à Tokyo.* Drinks auf dem Dach des Claska Hotels in Tokio.

150 Floating wood staircase, Junko Koshino's flat, Tokyo. *Escalier flottant en bois dans l'appartement de Junko Koshino, à Tokyo.* Frei schwebende Holztreppe in Junko Koshinos Wohnung in Tokio.

151 Another view of Koshino's staircase, Tokyo. *Autre vue de l'escalier, dans l'appartement de Junko Koshino, à Tokyo.* Eine weitere Perspektive der Treppe in Koshinos Wohnung in Tokio.

153 Quiet corner in the Koshino flat, Tokyo. *Petit coin tranquille dans l'appartement de Junko Koshino, à Tokyo.* Stilles Eckchen in Koshinos Wohnung in Tokio.

154 Wood and mirrors: bathroom of the Koshino flat. *Bois et miroirs : la salle de bain de l'appartement de Junko Koshino.* Holz und Spiegel: Badezimmer in Koshinos Wohnung.

155 Narrow staircase in Junko Koshino's flat, Tokyo. *Escalier étroit dans l'appartement de Junko Koshino, à Tokyo.* Eine schmale Treppe in Junko Koshinos Wohnung in Tokio.

156 Ready for tea ceremony, Koshino's flat, Tokyo. *Préparatifs pour la cérémonie du thé, dans l'appartement de Junko Koshino, à Tokyo.* Die Teezeremonie in Koshinos Wohnung in Tokio kann beginnen.

158 The tea ceremony room at Koshino's, Tokyo. *Salle consacrée à la cérémonie du thé, dans l'appartement de Koshino, à Tokyo.* Blick in den Raum in Koshinos Wohnung in Tokio, in dem die Teezeremonie stattfindet.

159 Recessed shelves hold antique ceramics at Koshino's. *Dans l'appartement de Koshino, des étagères recèlent un trésor de céramiques antique.* Kostbare antike Keramik schmückt die Einbauregale in Koshinos Wohnung.

160 Outdoor courtyard at Claska Hotel, Tokyo. *Cour extérieure de l'hôtel Claska, à Tokyo.* Kleiner Hof des Claska Hotels in Tokio.

161 Giant lantern: exterior of Masaki Endo's Natural Strips II house. *Lanterne géante : extérieur de la maison Natural Strips II de Masaki Endo.* Eine Riesenlaterne: Masaki Endos Natural-Strips-II-Haus.

162 Detail, architect Eizo Shiina's house in Tokyo. *Détail de la demeure de l'architecte Eizo Shiina, à Tokyo.* Detail, das Haus des Architekten Eizo Shiina in Tokio.

164 In the garden, Eizo Shiina's house, Tokyo. *Dans le jardin de la maison d'Eizo Shiina, à Tokyo.* Der Garten des Hauses von Eizo Shiina in Tokio.

165 Straw slippers on the balcony, Shiina's house, Tokyo. *Mules en paille sur le balcon de la maison d'Eizo Shiina, à Tokyo.* Strohsandalen auf dem Fensterbrett des Balkons in Shiinas Haus in Tokio.

167 Sunlight on fake "bamboo" plastic slats, Kuma's Plastic House. *Soleil à travers des lamelles de « bambou » en plastique de la Maison de Plastique de Kuma.* Sonnenlicht strömt durch die »Bambus«-Latten im Plastic House.

168 Glows like kryptonite: hallway at Plastic House, Tokyo. *Éclats de kryptonite : couloir de la Maison de Plastique, à Tokyo. Der Flur im Plastic House in Tokio leuchtet wie Krypton.*

169 Sunshine through plastic: overhead view, Plastic House, Tokyo. *Soleil à travers le plastique : vue de la Maison de Plastique, à Tokyo. Sonnenschein dringt durch den Kunststoff: Blick von oben auf das Plastic House.*

170 Man-made and hand-made: straw cassock at Plastic House, Tokyo. *Artificiel et artisanal : soutane de paille dans la Maison de Plastique, à Tokyo. Handgemacht: Ein geflochtener Hocker aus Stroh im Plastic House in Tokio.*

171 Plastic walls enclose the air conditioning system, Plastic House. *Des murs de plastique dissimulent la climatisation, sur le toit de la Maison de Plastique. Die Klimaanlage auf dem Dach des Plastic House wurde mit Kunststoffplatten umbaut.*

172 Noriko Kirishima, co-owner of Plastic House, and baby Kyra. *Noriko Kirishima, copropriétaire de la Maison de Plastique, avec son bébé Kyra. Noriko Kirishima, die Miteigentümerin des Plastic House, mit Baby Kyra.*

174 Narrow passage at Natural Strips II House, Tokyo. *Couloir étroit dans la maison de Masaki Endo, à Tokyo. Ein schmaler Gang im Natural-Strips-II-Haus in Tokio.*

175 Detail, bedroom at Masaki Endo's Natural Strips II. *Détail de la chambre, dans la maison de Masaki Endo. Detail, Schlafzimmer in Masaki Endos Natural-Strips-II-Haus.*

177 Tiny shrine at Endo's Natural Strips II house. *Reliquaire minuscule, dans la maison de Masaki Endo. Winziger Schrein in Endos Natural-Strips-II-Haus.*

178 A corner for meditation: Nakamura's house, Tokyo. *Coin méditation dans la demeure de Yoshifumi Nakamura, à Tokyo.* Ein Platz zum Meditieren in Nakamuras Haus in Tokio.

179 Outside looking in: Endo's Natural Strips II house, Tokyo. *Depuis l'extérieur, aperçu de l'intérieur de la maison de Masaki Endo.* Einblick von draußen in Endos Natural-Strips-II-Haus in Tokio.

180 Bath with a view: Kenzo Tange's Park Hyatt Hotel, Tokyo. *Salle de bain avec vue, dans l'hôtel Park Hyatt construit par Kenzo Tange, à Tokyo.* Badezimmer mit Aussicht in Kenzo Tanges Park Hyatt Hotel in Tokio.

182 The Sofitel Hotel, seen from the pond at Ueno Park. *L'hôtel Sofitel, depuis l'étang du parc Ueno.* Das Sofitel Hotel vom Teich im Ueno Park gesehen.

183 Swimming pool at the Park Hyatt Hotel, Tokyo. *La piscine de l'hôtel Park Hyatt de Tokyo.* Swimmingpool im Park Hyatt Hotel in Tokio.

185 Detail of the pyramid-shaped tower, Sofitel Hotel. *Détail de la tour en forme de pyramide de l'hôtel Sofitel.* Detail des pyramidenförmigen Turms, Sofitel Hotel.

187 Red blossoms brighten Endo's Natural Strips II house. *Des fleurs rouges égayent la demeure de Masaki Endo.* Rote Blüten bringen Farbe in Endos Natural-Strips-II-Haus.

Great Escapes Asia
Ed. Angelika Taschen, Christiane
Reiter / Hardcover, 400 pp. /
€ 29.99 / $ 39.99 / £ 19.99 /
¥ 5.900

Inside Asia
Ed. Angelika Taschen, Reto
Guntli, Sunil Sethi / Hardcover,
2 volumes 880 pp. / € 99.99 /
$ 125 / £ 69.99 / ¥ 15.000

"These books are beautiful objects, well-designed and lucid." —*Le Monde*, Paris, on the ICONS series

"Buy them all and add some pleasure to your life."

African Style
Ed. Angelika Taschen

Alchemy & Mysticism
Alexander Roob

American Indian
Dr. Sonja Schierle

Angels
Gilles Néret

Architecture Now!
Ed. Philip Jodidio

Art Now
Eds. Burkhard Riemschneider,
Uta Grosenick

Atget's Paris
Ed. Hans Christian Adam

Audrey Hepburn
Ed. Paul Duncan

Bamboo Style
Ed. Angelika Taschen

Berlin Style
Ed. Angelika Taschen

Brussels Style
Ed. Angelika Taschen

Cars of the 50s
Ed. Jim Heimann, Tony Thacker

Cars of the 60s
Ed. Jim Heimann, Tony Thacker

Cars of the 70s
Ed. Jim Heimann, Tony Thacker

Chairs
Charlotte & Peter Fiell

Charlie Chaplin
Ed. Paul Duncan

China Style
Ed. Angelika Taschen

Christmas
Ed. Jim Heimann, Steven Heller

Classic Rock Covers
Ed. Michael Ochs

Clint Eastwood
Ed. Paul Duncan

Design Handbook
Charlotte & Peter Fiell

Design of the 20th Century
Charlotte & Peter Fiell

Design for the 21st Century
Charlotte & Peter Fiell

Devils
Gilles Néret

Digital Beauties
Ed. Julius Wiedmann

Robert Doisneau
Ed. Jean-Claude Gautrand

East German Design
Ralf Ulrich / Photos: Ernst Hedler

Egypt Style
Ed. Angelika Taschen

Encyclopaedia Anatomica
Ed. Museo La Specola Florence

M.C. Escher

Fashion
Ed. The Kyoto Costume Institute

Fashion Now!
Ed. Terry Jones, Susie Rushton

Fruit
Ed. George Brookshaw,
Uta Pellgrü-Gagel

HR Giger
HR Giger

Grand Tour
Harry Seidler

Graphic Design
Eds. Charlotte & Peter Fiell

Greece Style
Ed. Angelika Taschen

Halloween
Ed. Jim Heimann, Steven Heller

Havana Style
Ed. Angelika Taschen

Homo Art
Gilles Néret

Hot Rods
Ed. Coco Shinomiya, Tony
Thacker

Hula
Ed. Jim Heimann

Indian Style
Ed. Angelika Taschen

India Bazaar
Samantha Harrison, Bari Kumar

Industrial Design
Charlotte & Peter Fiell

Japanese Beauties
Ed. Alex Gross

Las Vegas
Ed. Jim Heimann,
W. R. Wilkerson III

London Style
Ed. Angelika Taschen

Marilyn Monroe
Ed. Paul Duncan

Marlon Brando
Ed. Paul Duncan

Mexico Style
Ed. Angelika Taschen

Miami Style
Ed. Angelika Taschen

Minimal Style
Ed. Angelika Taschen

Morocco Style
Ed. Angelika Taschen

New York Style
Ed. Angelika Taschen

Orson Welles
Ed. Paul Duncan

Paris Style
Ed. Angelika Taschen

Penguin
Frans Lanting

20th Century Photography
Museum Ludwig Cologne

Photo Icons I
Hans-Michael Koetzle

Photo Icons II
Hans-Michael Koetzle

Pierre et Gilles
Eric Troncy

Provence Style
Ed. Angelika Taschen

Robots & Spaceships
Ed. Teruhisa Kitahara

Safari Style
Ed. Angelika Taschen

Seaside Style
Ed. Angelika Taschen

Signs
Ed. Julius Wiedman

South African Style
Ed. Angelika Taschen

Starck
Philippe Starck

Surfing
Ed. Jim Heimann

Sweden Style
Ed. Angelika Taschen

Sydney Style
Ed. Angelika Taschen

Tattoos
Ed. Henk Schiffmacher

Tiffany
Jacob Baal-Teshuva

Tiki Style
Sven Kirsten

Tokyo Style
Ed. Angelika Taschen

Tuscany Style
Ed. Angelika Taschen

Valentines
Ed. Jim Heimann,
Steven Heller

Web Design: Best Studios
Ed. Julius Wiedemann

Web Design: E-Commerce
Ed. Julius Wiedemann

Web Design: Flash Sites
Ed. Julius Wiedemann

Web Design: Music Sites
Ed. Julius Wiedemann

Web Design: Portfolios
Ed. Julius Wiedemann

Women Artists
in the 20th and 21st Century
Ed. Uta Grosenick

70s Fashion
Ed. Jim Heimann

ICONS